West Virginia
The Mountain State

Robin Koontz

PowerKiDS
press™
New York

To my mom, for dragging us to Coolfont in 1966

Published in 2011 by The Rosen Publishing Group, Inc.
29 East 21st Street, New York, NY 10010

First Edition

Editor: Amelie von Zumbusch
Book Design: Greg Tucker
Layout Design: Ashley Burrell
Photo Researcher: Jessica Gerweck

Photo Credits: Cover, p. 17, 22 (bird) Shutterstock.com; p. 5 Harrison Shull/Getty Images; p. 7 © North Wind Picture Archives; p. 9 MPI/ Getty Images; p. 11 Willard Clay/Getty Images; p. 13 Stephen J. Krasemann/Getty Images; p. 15 Joe Sohm/Getty Images; p. 19 Skip Brown/Getty Images; p. 22 (tree) © www.iStockphoto.com/Jim Jurica; p. 22 (bear) © www.iStockphoto.com/Suzann Julien; p. 22 (flower) Wikimedia Commons; p. 22 (Pearl Buck) Arnold Genthe/Getty Images; p. 22 (Chuck Yeager) Hulton Archive/Getty Images; p. 22 (Randy Moss) G. Fiume/Getty Images.

Library of Congress Cataloging-in-Publication Data

Koontz, Robin Michal.
  West Virginia : the Mountain State / Robin Koontz. — 1st ed.
      p. cm. — (Our amazing states)
  Includes index.
  ISBN 978-1-4488-0652-2 (library binding) — ISBN 978-1-4488-0736-9 (pbk.) — ISBN 978-1-4488-0737-6 (6-pack)
  1. West Virginia—Juvenile literature. I. Title.
  F241.3.K66 2011
  975.4—dc22
                                                    2009054328
Manufactured in the United States of America

CPSIA Compliance Information: Batch #WS10PK: For Further Information contact Rosen Publishing, New York, New York at 1-800-237-9932

Contents

The Mountain State

West Virginia is known as the Mountain State. Mountains make up more of the land there than they do in any other eastern state. It is hard to find any large, flat places in West Virginia! The mountains in West Virginia are part of the Appalachian **mountain system**. This mountain system includes lots of mountains, hills, and **plateaus**. It crosses through many states in the eastern United States.

For many years, the mountains cut the people living in the Appalachians off from the people in the nearby places. The people in the mountains became known as Appalachians. They had their own way of life. Today, their art, music, food, and **traditions** are still alive in West Virginia.

4

West Virginia's mountains are a great place to hike. Hikers there can enjoy beautiful views and see the state's great natural beauty.

Early Life

In the past, people from several native **cultures** lived and hunted in West Virginia. By the 1600s, many Indian groups lived there. At that time, English people settled in the Virginia **Colony**, to the east. Soon, colonists moved west. Indians destroyed many English settlements. They were angry that the colonists had taken over their land.

In the 1770s, Virginia and other colonies broke away from England. Virginia became part of the United States. Most people in western Virginia had small family farms. Eastern Virginia's farmers had big farms. They controlled Virginia's government. They passed laws that helped them but not the western farmers. The western farmers became upset about this.

Many of the first English settlers in West Virginia lived in small homes like this one. The cliffs behind the house are the state's striking Seneca Rocks.

A Sad Time

Many farmers in eastern Virginia had African-American **slaves** working on their farms. However, slaves were uncommon in western Virginia. Across the United States, people disagreed about slavery. John Brown was a man who fought to end slavery. In 1859, he and his men took over the national **armory** in Harpers Ferry, in western Virginia. Brown was caught and hanged. However, he became a hero to the people who wanted to end slavery.

In 1861, the Civil War began. Several states that had slavery decided to form their own country. Virginia was one of these states. However, people in western Virginia did not want to be part of the new country. On June 20, 1863, they broke away from Virginia and became the thirty-fifth U.S. state.

John Brown and his men took over the Harpers Ferry armory on October 16, 1859. Two days later, American soldiers fought to take it back. Here the soldiers are storming the armory.

Mountains and Rivers

West Virginia is shaped kind of like a bug with two arms, which point north and east. The arms are called panhandles. The northern part of the Blue Ridge Mountains is in the eastern panhandle. Mountains, hills, plateaus, and rivers cover most of the state. The Ohio River is part of the western border of West Virginia. The Potomac River forms part of the northern border.

The Allegheny Mountains are also in West Virginia. These mountains have more than 40 **peaks**. It rains heavily there. This makes the Allegheny Mountains the wettest part of the state. The rainwater feeds the rivers and streams. The weather in West Virginia is usually mild, but winters in the mountains can be very cold!

Some of West Virginia's rivers have rapids and beautiful waterfalls. Blackwater Falls, seen here, are on the Blackwater River. They are in West Virginia's Blackwater Falls State Park.

Wild and Wonderful

The woods in West Virginia are filled with trees such as hickory, poplar, pine, oak, locust, and cherry. Virginia creeper vines twist up the trees. The vines can be strong enough to swing on! Flowering bushes, called **rhododendrons**, grow in the shade. Wildflowers, such as fireweed, buttercups, ladyslippers, lillies of the valley, and black-eyed Susans, flower in the spring and summer.

West Virginia is home to many animals. The state's nuts, berries, and roots are favorite foods of the black bear. Black bears are often black. However, they can also be brown, tan, or gray. They share the land with animals such as deer, rabbits, skunks, and flying squirrels. There are also many different kinds of frogs, fish, insects, and birds.

The black bear is West Virginia's state animal. Black bear mothers, such as this one, take good care of their cubs. They feed them, keep them warm, and chase away enemies.

Nature's Gifts

West Virginia makes most of its money through services like health care. People also mine coal. Coal is found across West Virginia. It is used for **energy**. Thousands of people work in the state's coal mines. Clay, salt, and sandstone are also mined there. **Natural gas** is found there, too.

Sand from West Virginia is used to make glass. Glass factories make many glass things, including marbles. Marble King, in Paden City, West Virginia, makes more than a million marbles a day!

Much of West Virginia's soil has rock called limestone in it. The limestone makes West Virginia a good place to grow crops. Many farms also raise chickens and cows. Limestone is used to make roads, too.

After it is mined, coal must be brought to a power plant. There, it is burned to produce electricity. These barges on the Kanawha River, in West Virginia, are carrying coal.

City on the River

Charleston became the capital of West Virginia in 1885. It is also the state's biggest city. Charleston is in the Kanawha Valley. There is coal and natural gas nearby. The Kanawha River flows through the city. There are many companies based in Charleston. The city has a lot of factories, too. It is also home to West Virginia State College.

Charleston has lots of fun places to visit. People can learn about the state's history there. One of the oldest roads in West Virginia is the Midland Trail. It winds through Charleston and across south central West Virginia. There are historic places all along the way. People can stop along the road to hike and bicycle. They can go swimming and boating in the rivers, too.

The West Virginia capitol, seen here, was built between 1924 and 1932. The big building has more than 300 rooms. It also has a huge gold dome.

The Mon

The Monongahela National Forest is in the highlands of West Virginia. It covers almost 1 million acres (404,686 ha). The Mon, as it is called, has hundreds of miles (km) of trails. It also has rivers and streams with waterfalls. There are steep cliffs, caves, and beautiful forests. People camp in the forest's campgrounds. They have picnics there, too. Visitors hike, bike, fish, and watch the wildlife.

Many smaller parks are part of the Mon. For example, Spruce Knob-Seneca Rocks National Recreation Area is there. It has the highest point in West Virginia. People climb the rocks and enjoy the beautiful views. Sometimes, they see the remains of the mountain farms that once dotted the hills.

These people are mountain biking through Monongahela National Forest. They are on the beautiful Props Run Trail, near Slatyfork, West Virginia.

Wonderful West Virginia

People who hike and bike love West Virginia. The Appalachian Trail runs through the state. The trail is more than 2,000 miles (3,219 km) long. It winds through 14 eastern states.

In the past, trains chugged up and down West Virginia's mountains. They carried logs to sawmills, where the logs were cut up. Today, some railroad tracks have been turned into hiking, biking, and horseback-riding trails. They are called rail trails.

West Virginia has several **mineral** springs. Berkeley Springs, West Virginia, is known for its warm springs. People can soak in the springs year-round. Visitors can also enjoy local music, festivals, and crafts there. There are lots of things to do in West Virginia!

armory (ARM-ree) A place where arms are stored.

colony (KAH-luh-nee) A new place where people move that is still ruled by the leaders of the country from which they came.

cultures (KUL-churz) Groups of people with shared beliefs, practices, and arts.

energy (EH-ner-jee) The power to work or to act.

mineral (MIN-rul) A natural thing that is not an animal, a plant, or another living thing.

mountain system (MOWN-tun SIS-tem) A group of mountains and hills that all run together.

natural gas (NA-chuh-rul GAS) A kind of gas that is found in the ground and can be burned to produce electricity.

peaks (PEEKS) The tops of mountains.

plateaus (pla-TOHZ) Broad, flat, high pieces of land.

rhododendrons (roh-duh-DEN-drenz) Trees or bushes with pink, white, or purple flowers.

slaves (SLAYVZ) People who are "owned" by another person and forced to work for him or her.

traditions (truh-DIH-shunz) Ways of doing things that have been passed down over time.

West Virginia State Symbols

State Tree
Sugar Maple

State Animal
Black Bear

State Flag

State Bird
Cardinal

State Flower
Rhododendron

State Seal

Famous People from West Virginia

Pearl Buck
(1892–1973)
Born in Hillsboro, WV
Author

Chuck Yeager
(1923–)
Born in Myra, WV
Pilot and General

Randy Moss
(1977–)
Born in Rand, WV
Football Player

22

West Virginia State Map

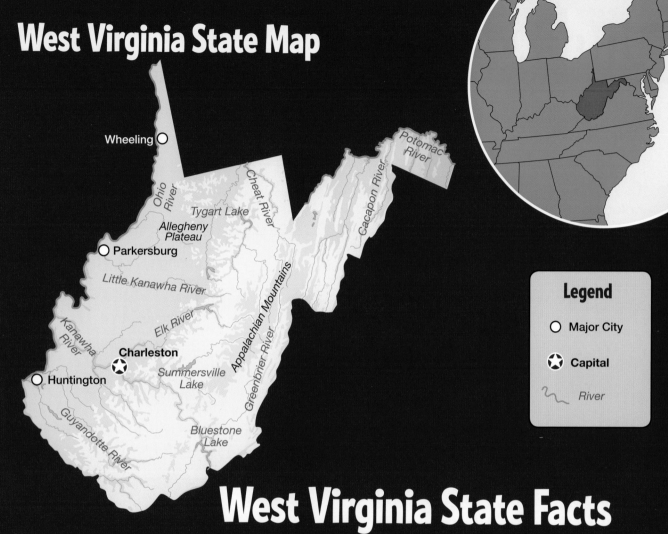

Wheeling ○

Ohio River

Cheat River

Potomac River

Tygart Lake

Cacapon River

Allegheny Plateau

Parkersburg ○

Little Kanawha River

Appalachian Mountains

Greenbrier River

Elk River

Kanawha River

Charleston ☆

Summersville Lake

Huntington ○

Guyandotte River

Bluestone Lake

Legend

○ Major City

☆ Capital

〜 River

West Virginia State Facts

Population: About 1,808,344

Area: 24,181 square miles (62,629 sq km)

Motto: "Montani Semper Liberi" ("Mountaineers Are Always Free")

Songs: "The West Virginia Hills," words by Ellen King and music by H. E. Engle, "West Virginia, My Home Sweet Home," words and music by Julian G. Hearne, Jr., and "This Is My West Virginia," words and music by Iris Bell

Index

Web Sites

Due to the changing nature of Internet links, PowerKids Press has developed an online list of Web sites related to the subject of this book. This site is updated regularly. Please use this link to access the list:
www.powerkidslinks.com/amst/wv/